D0974988

MARK TWAIN'S
TRADE MARK
WIT & WISDOM

THE WIT AND WISDOM OF

Mark Twain

EDITED BY AARON JOHN LOEB

FALL RIVER PRESS

New York

FALL RIVER PRESS

New York

An Imprint of Sterling Publishing
387 Park Avenue South
New York, NY 10016

Book design by Rich Hazelton
Illustrations by Paul Hoffman

ISBN: 978-1-4351-4431-6 (print format)
ISBN: 978-1-4351-4432-3 (ebook)

Distributed in Canada by Sterling Publishing
c/o Canadian Manda Group, 165 Dufferin Street
Toronto, Ontario, Canada M6K 3H6
Distributed in the United Kingdom by GMC Distribution Services
Castle Place, 166 High Street, Lewes, East Sussex, England BN7 1XU
Distributed in Australia by Capricorn Link (Australia) Pty. Ltd.
P.O. Box 704, Windsor, NSW 2756, Australia

For information about custom editions, special sales, and premium and
corporate purchases, please contact Sterling Special Sales at 800-805-5489
or specialsales@sterlingpublishing.com.

Manufactured in the United States of America

2 4 6 8 10 9 7 5 3 1

www.sterlingpublishing.com

CONTENTS

INTRODUCTION

Compiling *The Wit & Wisdom of Mark Twain* presented an exacting challenge: How to include everything we found deliciously on target? Twain waxed witty and wise so often that it was difficult to choose which paragraphs, sentences, and turns of phrase best deserved to be in the book. Difficult, but not impossible. What we needed were a few guidelines.

The variety of Twain's work is staggering. He wrote novels, travel sketches, short stories, and essays. He delivered countless speeches. He even penned a play or two. Much of this work remains little read in comparison with his fantastically popular novels. However, Twain's short works are often funnier and more pithy than his famous novels. One guideline in assembling this book was to extract Twain gems from as diverse a collection of sources as possible—from the renowned and reputed "The reports of my death are greatly exaggerated" to less familiar, but no less humorous, witticisms. The result is a book that will not only serve as a delightful reference, but also as a sort of pocket penlight leading the way to Twain's less often admired baubles.

The second guideline regarded length. Exploring the texts revealed that Twain's "sprints" are often wittier than his "marathons." Bearing this in mind, we have kept Twain's words to their effective and resounding essence, allowing us to offer even more of the incomparable Mr. Clemens. As a by-product of this Spartan choice—rejecting, with one notable exception, the bludgeon of lengthier excerpts in favor of the rapier of the comic thrust—the book becomes a perfect pick-me-up, something that can be easily read straight through or browsed for a couple of minutes at a time.

In the end, we decided to distribute this bounty among the general categories that seemed most appropriate—Twain on money, on death, on travel, on politics, on the art of writing, and so on. But we think the reader will quickly learn that Twain's verbal assaults can send shock waves in many directions at once. A long-winded politician could not safely read the section on writing, nor could a foreigner read Twain's comments on America, without feeling the sting that is, presumably, aimed elsewhere. While, on the human condition—our largest category and the one that exempts no one—Twain has said more—and said it better—than almost anybody.

A final decision dealt with presentation. Unlike Benjamin Franklin, Twain's wisest remarks are not neatly packaged in tiny containers, but sit like land mines under the rich topsoil of his prose. Therefore, many of the quotable remarks herein are introduced—briefly, we hope—by a sentence or phrase that establishes the original context within which Twain's barb was delivered. Following the quote comes its source, though in the spirit of keeping this book loose and light-hearted we have not differentiated between the various genres of the source works (novels, stories, speeches, essays, etc.), contenting ourselves to give only the tide of the particular piece. An attributed quote has been included only if there were two sources claiming Twain as its author. Though in fairness it must be said that clever remarks stuck to Twain like lint to a new suit.

Over eighty years after his bodily death, Mark Twain lives on. So he was right once again: Reports of his death have been greatly exaggerated. In fact, they're a downright lie. To discover this, reader, simply read on. The explanations are now ended. The true wit and wisdom awaits.

—Aaron John Loeb, 1996

Mark Twain

On Love, Friendship, and Family

Always obey your parents, when they are present.

Advice to Youth

I seldom said anything smart when I was a child. I tried it once or twice, but it was not popular.

Wit Inspirations of the "Two-Year-Olds"

{TWAIN ON ONE OF HIS ANCESTORS, AUGUSTUS TWAIN} He was as full of fun as he could be, and used to take his old saber and sharpen it up, and get in a convenient place on a dark night, and stick it through people as they went by, to see them jump. He was a born humorist.

A Burlesque Biography

{TWAIN'S ADVICE TO LITTLE GIRLS} If at any time you find it necessary to correct your brother, do not correct him with mud—never, on any account, throw mud at him, because it will spoil his clothes. It is better to scald him a little, for then you obtain desirable results.

Advice to Little Girls

{DISCUSSING ONE OF HIS RELATIVES, WHO DIED IMMEDIATELY AFTER INHERITING AN EARLDOM IN ENGLAND} This has always been the way with our family. They always die when they could make anything by not doing it.

Mental Telegraphy

My father was a St. Bernard, my mother was a Collie, but I am a Presbyterian.

A Dog's Tale

The fair record of my life has been tarnished by just one pun. My father overheard that, and he hunted me over four or five townships seeking to take my life.

Wit Inspirations of the "Two-Year-Olds"

{SUPPOSED ADVICE FROM BRIGHAM YOUNG} In a small family, and in a small family only, you will find that comfort and that peace of mind which are the best at last of the blessings this world is able to afford us. . . . Take my word for it, ten or eleven wives is all you need—never go over it.

Roughing It

{AN IMAGINARY CONVERSATION BETWEEN NAPOLEON AND TWAIN}
Napoleon: I suppose life can never get entirely dull to an American, because whenever he can't strike up any other way to put in his time he can always get away with a few years trying to find out who his grandfather was!
Twain: Right, your excellency! But I reckon a Frenchman's got his little stand-by for a dull time, too; because when all other interests fail he can turn in and see if he can't figure out who his father was!

What Paul Bourget Thinks of Us

The first year of marriage [is] the most trying year for any young couple, for then the mutual failings are coming one by one to light, and the necessary adjustments are being made in pain and tribulation.

In Defense of Harriet Shelley

Women cannot receive even the most palpably judicious suggestion without arguing it; that is, married women.

Experience of the McWilliamses with Membranous Croup

Familiarity breeds contempt—and children.

Notebook

One frequently only finds out how really beautiful a really beautiful woman is after considerable acquaintance with her . . .

Innocents Abroad

{ON THE "MODEL BOY" IN HIS HOME TOWN} He was the admiration of all the mothers and the detestation of all their sons.

Life on the Mississippi

It is very difficult to take compliments. I do not care whether you deserve them or not, it is just as difficult to take them.

Compliments and Degrees

Things ne'er do go smoothly in weddings, suicides, or courtships.

On Poetry, Veracity, and Suicide

{ATTRIBUTED BY TWAIN TO TOM REED, BUT TWAIN WAS PROBABLY PUTTING WORDS IN HIS MOUTH} Some of us can't be optimists, but by judiciously utilizing the opportunities that Providence puts in our way we can all be bigamists.

Sixty-Seventh Birthday

Man will do many things to get himself loved, he will do all things to get himself envied.

Following the Equator

You can't reason with your heart; it has its own laws, and thumps about things which the intellect scorns.

A Connecticut Yankee in King Arthur's Court

Grief can take care of itself; but to get the full value of a joy you must have somebody to divide it with.

Following the Equator

Love is a madness; if thwarted it develops fast.

A Memorable Assassination

To be human is to have one's little modicum of romance secreted away in one's composition. One never ceases to make a hero of one's self—in private.

The Gilded Age

When I was a boy of fourteen, my father was so ignorant I could hardly stand to have the old man around. But when I got to be twenty-one, I was astonished at how much he had learned in seven years.

Attributed

I have found out that there ain't no surer way to find out whether you like people or hate them than to travel with them.

Tom Sawyer Abroad

I have been complimented myself a great many times, and they always embarrass me—I always feel that they have not said enough.

Fulton Day, Jamestown

{RESPONDING TO THE POPULAR TREND OF PUBLISHING THE WITTICISMS OF CHILDREN} Judging by the average published specimens of smart sayings, the rising generation of children are little better than idiots.

Wit Inspirations of the "Two-Year-Olds"

They say that you can't live by bread alone, but I can live on compliments.

Compliments and Degrees

When people do not respect us we are sharply offended; yet in his private heart no man much respects himself.

Following the Equator

On the Human Condition (and Other Afflictions)

I find that principles have no real force except when one is well fed.

Adam's Diary

He was a good doctor, and a good man, and he had a good heart, but one had to know him a year to get over hating him.

Was It Heaven? Or Hell?

How easy it is to go from bad to worse, when once we have started upon a downward course!

The $30,000 Bequest

I have criticized absent people so often, and then discovered, to my humiliation, that I was talking with their relatives, that I have grown superstitious about that sort of thing and dropped it.

A Manuscript with a History

Nothing so needs reforming as other people's habits.

Pudd'nhead Wilson

It were not best that we should all think alike; it is difference of opinion that makes horse-races.

Pudd'nhead Wilson

We can secure other people's approval if we do right and try hard; but our own is worth a hundred of it, and no way has been found out of securing that.

Following the Equator

Necessarily we are all fond of murders, scandals, swindles, robberies, explosions, collisions, and all such things, when we know the people, and when they are neighbors and friends, but when they are strangers we do not get any great pleasure out of them, as a rule.

Italian without a Master

The human being's first duty . . . is to think about himself until he has exhausted the subject, then he is in a condition to take up minor interests and think of other people.

Was It Heaven? Or Hell?

The average man is what his environment and his superstitions have made him; and their function is to make him an ass.

At the Appetite Cure

There is no variety in the human race. We are all children, all children of the one Adam, and we love toys.

Does the Race of Man Love a Lord?

Shabbiness and dishonesty are not the monopoly of any race or creed, but are merely human.

Concerning the Jews

Good breeding consists in concealing how much we think of ourselves and how little we think of other persons.

Notebook

It takes your enemy and your friend, working together, to hurt you to the heart; the one to slander you and the other to get the news to you.

Following the Equator

Adam was but human—this explains it all. He did not want the apple for the apple's sake, he wanted it only because it was forbidden. The mistake was in not forbidding the serpent; then he would have eaten the serpent.

Pudd'nhead Wilson

Man is the only animal that blushes. Or needs to.

Following the Equator

The most valuable thing in the world is the homage of men, whether deserved or undeserved.

At the Shrine of Saint Wagner

By trying we can easily learn to endure adversity. Another man's, I mean.

Following the Equator

Barring that natural expression of villainy which we all have, the man looked honest enough.

A Mysterious Visit

{Twain's advice to the young} If a person offend you, and you are in doubt as to whether it was intentional or not, do not resort to extreme measures; simply watch your chance and hit him with a brick.

Advice to Youth

The history of our race, and each individual's experience, are sown thick with evidence that a truth is not hard to kill and that a lie told well is immortal.

Advice to Youth

I think that all this courteous lying is a sweet and loving art, and should be cultivated. The highest perfection of politeness is only a beautiful edifice, built, from the base to the dome, of graceful and gilded forms of charitable and unselfish lying.

On the Decaying Art of Lying

There's a good spot tucked away somewhere in everybody. You'll be a long time finding it, sometimes.

Refuge of the Derelicts

Don't you know that the very thing a man dreads is the thing that always happens?

Roughing It

{ON WOMANKIND} It is her blessed mission to comfort the sorrowing, plead for the erring, encourage the faint of purpose, succor the distressed, uplift the fallen, befriend the friendless—in a word, afford the healing of her sympathies and a home in her heart for all the bruised and persecuted children of misfortune that knock at its hospitable door.

Speech at the Scottish Banquet

We do not deal much in facts when we are contemplating ourselves.

Does the Race of Man Love a Lord?

Nothing that grieves us can be called little: by the eternal laws of proportion a child's loss of a doll and a king's loss of a crown are events of the same size.

Which Was the Dream?

An enemy can partly ruin a man, but it takes a good-natured injudicious friend to complete the thing and make it perfect.

Pudd'nhead Wilson

Like most other people, I often feel mean, and act accordingly . . .

Curing a Cold

There is no character, howsoever good and fine, but it can be destroyed by ridicule, howsoever poor and witless.

Pudd'nhead Wilson

Courage is resistance to fear, mastery of fear—not absence of fear.

Pudd'nhead Wilson

There are people who think that honesty is always the best policy. This is superstition: there are times when the appearance of it is worth six of it.

Attributed

A lie can travel halfway around the world while the truth is putting on its shoes.

Attributed

Gratitude and treachery are merely the two extremities of the same procession.

Pudd'nhead Wilson

It is often the case that the man who can't tell a lie thinks he is the best judge of one.

Pudd'nhead Wilson

Repartee is something we think of twenty-four hours too late.

Attributed

If you pick up a starving dog and make him prosperous, he will not bite you. This is the principal difference between a dog and a man.

Pudd'nhead Wilson

One is apt to overestimate beauty when it is rare.

Innocents Abroad

The universal brotherhood of man is our most precious possession, what there is of it.

Following the Equator

There are several good protections against temptations but the surest is cowardice.

Following the Equator

When ill luck begins, it does not come in sprinkles, but in showers.

Pudd'nhead Wilson

I cannot always be cheerful, and I cannot always be chaffing; I must sometimes lay the cap and bells aside, and recognize that I am of the human race like the rest, and must have my cares and griefs.

Books, Authors, and Hats

A certain amount of pride always goes along with a teaspoonful of brains . . . and admirers had often told me I had nearly a basketful [of brains]—though they were rather reserved as to the size of the basket.

Unconscious Plagiarism

{TWAIN ON WOMANKIND} As a sweetheart, she has few equals and no superiors; as a cousin, she is convenient; as a wealthy grandmother with an incurable distemper, she is precious; as a wet-nurse she has no equal among men.

Woman—An Opinion

April 1. This is the day upon which we are reminded of what we are on the other three hundred and sixty-four.

Pudd'nhead Wilson

When we are young we generally estimate an opinion by the size of the person that holds it, but later we find that that is an uncertain rule, for we realize that there are times when a hornet's opinion disturbs us more than an emperor's.

An Undelivered Speech

The older we grow the greater becomes our wonder at how much ignorance one can contain without bursting one's clothes.

University Settlement Society

Human nature is so constructed, we are so persistent, that when we know that we are born to a thing we do not care what the world thinks about it.

Henry Irving

Consider well the proportions of things. It is better to be a young June-bug than an old bird of paradise.

Pudd'nhead Wilson

One must keep up one's character. Earn a character first if you can, and if you can't; then assume one.

General Miles and the Dog

The rule is perfect: in all matters of opinion our adversaries are insane.

Christian Science

A human being has a natural desire to have more of a good thing than he needs.

Following the Equator

Everyone is a moon, and has a dark side which he never shows to anybody.

Following the Equator

It is easier to manufacture seven facts than one emotion.

Life on the Mississippi

In order to make a man or a boy covet a thing, it is only necessary to make the thing difficult to attain.

The Adventures of Tom Sawyer

I would not give the assassination of one personal friend for a whole massacre of [strangers]. And, to my mind, one relative or neighbor mixed up in a scandal is more interesting than a whole Sodom and Gomorrah of outlanders gone rotten.

Italian without a Master

The way it is now, the asylums can hold the sane people, but if we tried to shut up the insane we should run out of building materials.

Following the Equator

⊰⊱

A man has no business to be depressed by a disappointment . . . he ought to make up his mind to get even.

A Connecticut Yankee in King Arthur's Court

⊰⊱

Let us be thankful for the fools. But for them the rest of us could not succeed.

Following the Equator

⊰⊱

He was well born, as the saying is, and that's worth as much in a man as it is in a horse.

The Adventures of Huckleberry Finn

⊰⊱

I can stand any society. All that I care to know is that a man is a human being—that is enough for me; he can't be any worse.

Concerning the Jews

{WHEN ASKED WHAT TRAIT HE MOST DETESTED IN PEOPLE} That "trait" which you put "or" to to describe its possessor. {HE LATER WROTE OF HIS RESPONSE} I have to explain it every single time— "TRAIT-OR." I should think a fine cultivated intellect might guess that without any help.

Mental Photographs

I was born modest; not all over, but in spots.

A Connecticut Yankee in King Arthur's Court

We all like to see people sea-sick when we are not ourselves.

Innocents Abroad

It is the first wrong steps that count.

The $30,000 Bequest

Man is the Reasoning Animal. Such is the claim. I think it is open to dispute.

The Lowest Animal

Monarchies, aristocracies, and religions are all based upon that large defect in your race—the individual's distrust of his neighbor, and his desire, for safety's or comfort's sake, to stand well in his neighbor's eye.

The Mysterious Stranger

Eternal vigilance is the price of supremacy.

Eve's Diary

Happiness ain't a thing in itself—it's only a contrast with something that ain't pleasant.

Captain Stormfield's Visit to Heaven

There it is: it doesn't make any difference who we are or what we are, there's always somebody to look down on.

3,000 Years among the Microbes

To promise not to do a thing is the surest way in the world to make a body want to go and do that very thing.

The Adventures of Tom Sawyer

On the
Almighty Dollar

A dollar picked up in the road is more satisfying to you than the ninety-and-nine which you had to work for . . .

At the Shrine of Saint Wagner

The less a man knows the bigger the noise he makes and the higher the salary he commands.

How I Edited an Agricultural Paper

{RESPONDING TO A FRIEND'S ACCUSATION THAT A WEALTHY INDUSTRIALIST'S MONEY WAS TAINTED} That's right. 'Taint yours, and 'taint mine.

Attributed

{A RICH UNCLE LEAVES HIS NEPHEW, SALLY, A GREAT SUM OF MONEY} Tilbury now wrote to Sally, saying he should shortly die, and should leave him thirty thousand dollars, cash; not for love, but because money had given him most of his troubles and exasperations, and he wished to place it where there was good hope that it would continue its malignant work.

The $30,000 Bequest

Whenever a poor wretch asks you for help, and you feel a doubt as to what result may flow from your benevolence, give yourself the benefit of the doubt and kill the applicant.

About Magnanimous-Incident Literature

Whereas principle is a great and noble protection against showy and degrading vanities and vices, poverty is worth six of it.

The $30,000 Bequest

A banker is a fellow who lends you his umbrella when the sun is shining and wants it back the minute it begins to rain.

Attributed

Ever since I have been a director in an accident-insurance company I have felt that I am a better man. . . . I look upon a cripple now with affectionate interest—as an advertisement. I do not seem to care for poetry any more. I do not care for politics—even agriculture does not excite me. But to me now there is a charm about a railway collision that is unspeakable.

Speech on Accident Insurance

Many a small thing has been made large by the right kind of advertising.

A Connecticut Yankee in King Arthur's Court

Let us not be too particular; it is better to have old second-hand diamonds than none at all.

Following the Equator

Remember the poor—it costs nothing.

Attributed

There are two times in a man's life when he shouldn't speculate: when he can't afford it, and when he can.

Following the Equator

The holy passion of Friendship is of so sweet and steady and loyal and enduring a nature that it will last through a whole lifetime, if not asked to lend money.

Pudd'nhead Wilson

I wonder how much it would take to buy a soap-bubble, if there was only one in the world.

A Tramp Abroad

October. This is one of the peculiarly dangerous months to speculate in stocks in. The others are July, January, September, April, November, May, March, June, December, August, and February.

Pudd'nhead Wilson

Behold, the fool saith, "Put not all thine eggs in one basket"— which is but a manner of saying, "Scatter your money and your attention"; but the wise man saith, "Put all your eggs in one basket and—WATCH THAT BASKET."

Pudd'nhead Wilson

The poor are always good to the poor. When a person with his millions gives a hundred thousand dollars it makes a great noise in the world, but he does not miss it; it's the widow's mite that makes no noise but does the best work.

Votes for Women

All my life I have been honest—comparatively honest. I could never use money I had not made honestly—I could only lend it.

General Miles and the Dog

I don't know of a single foreign product that enters this country untaxed except the answer to prayer.

When in Doubt, Tell the Truth

Virtue has never been as respectable as money.

Innocents Abroad

When the average man mentions the name of a multimillionaire he does it with that mixture in his voice of awe and reverence and lust which burns in a Frenchman's eye when it falls on another man's centime.

Concerning the Jews

Prosperity is the best protector of principle.

Following the Equator

A man pretty much always refuses another man's first offer, no matter what it is.

The Gilded Age

Beautiful credit! The foundation of modern society.

The Gilded Age

Make money and the whole world will conspire to call you a gentleman.

Attributed

Few of us can stand prosperity—another man's, I mean.

Following the Equator

The world seems to think that the love of money is "American"; and that the mad desire to get rich suddenly is "American." I believe that both of these things are merely and broadly human, not American monopolies at all. The love of money is natural to all nations, for money is a good and strong friend.

What Paul Bourget Thinks of Us

He was a very inferior farmer when he first began, but a prolonged and unflinching assault upon his agricultural difficulties has had its effect at last, and he is now fast rising from affluence to poverty.

Rev. Henry Ward Beecher's Farm

Vast wealth, to the person unaccustomed to it, is a bane. It eats into the flesh and bone of his morals.

The $30,000 Bequest

The lack of money is the root of all evil.

More Maxims of Mark

Mark Twain

On Religion
and Morals

We ought never to do wrong when people are looking.

Double-Barreled Detective Story

History shows us that the Moral Sense enables us to perceive morality and how to avoid it, and that the Immoral Sense enables us to perceive immorality and how to enjoy it.

Following the Equator

Even the angels dislike a foreigner.

Concerning the Jews

There are not books enough on earth to contain the record of the prophecies Indians and other unauthorized parties have made; but one may carry in his overcoat pockets the record of all the prophecies that have been fulfilled.

A Burlesque Biography

Always do right. This will gratify some people, and astonish the rest.

Attributed

We do confess in public that we are the noblest work of
God, being moved to it by long habit, and teaching, and
superstition; but deep down in the secret places of our souls we
recognize that, if we are the noblest work, the less said about it
the better.

Does the Race of Man Love a Lord?

{RESPONDING TO PAUL BOURGET'S ANALYSIS OF AMERICAN CULTURE}
What would . . . France teach us? . . . Morals? No, we cannot
rob the poor to enrich ourselves.

What Paul Bourget Thinks of Us

Adam and Eve had many advantages, but the principal one was,
that they escaped teething.

Pudd'nhead Wilson

We have infinite trouble in solving man-made mysteries; it is
only when we set out to discover the secret of God that our
difficulties disappear.

As Concerns Interpreting the Deity

Morals are an acquirement—like music, like a foreign language, like piety, poker, paralysis—no man is born with them.

Seventieth Birthday

I cannot call to mind a single instance where I have ever been irreverent, except toward the things which were sacred to other people.

Is Shakespeare Dead?

Do I seem to be preaching? It is out of my line: I only do it because the rest of the clergy seem to be on vacation.

About Play Acting

Eternal Rest sounds comforting in the pulpit. . . . Well, you try it once, and see how heavy time will hang on your hands.

Captain Stormfield's Visit to Heaven

The Christian Bible is a drug store. Its contents remain the same; but the medical practice changes.

Bible Teaching and Religious Practice

Sometimes an ordained minister sets out to be blasphemous.
When this happens, the layman is out of the running; he
stands no chance.

To the Person Sitting in Darkness

The moral sense teaches us what is right, and how to avoid it—
when unpopular.

The United States of Lyncherdom

I haven't a particle of confidence in a man who has no redeeming
petty vices.

Letter

We were good Presbyterian boys when the weather was
doubtful; when it was fair we did wander a little from the fold.

Sixty-Seventh Birthday

Often it does seem such a pity that Noah didn't miss the boat.

Christian Science

Man is the Religious Animal. He is the only Religious
Animal. He is the only animal that has the True Religion—
several of them.

The Lowest Animal

Be careless in your dress if you must, but keep a tidy soul.

Following the Equator

If the man doesn't believe as we do, we say he is a crank, and
that settles it. I mean, it does nowadays, because now we can't
burn him.

Following the Equator

The church is always trying to get other people to reform;
it might not be a bad idea to reform itself a little by way
of example.

A Tramp Abroad

Principles is another name for prejudices.

Speech on Literature

A man is accepted into a church for what he believes and he is turned out for what he knows.

Attributed

{TWAIN TOLD A STORY OF A CONDEMNED MAN WHO ASKED A CLERGYMAN WHICH PLACE WAS THE BEST PLACE TO GO AFTER DEATH} The minister told him that each place had its advantages— heaven for climate, and hell for society.

Tammany and Crocker

{TWAIN AND HIS COMPANIONS WERE SHOCKED AT THE COST OF HIRING A BOAT ON THE SEA OF GALILEE} Do you wonder now that Christ walked?

Innocents Abroad

Two or three centuries from now it will be recognized that all the competent killers are Christians; then the pagan world will go to school to the Christian—not to acquire his religion, but his guns.

The Mysterious Stranger

In the first place God made idiots. This was for practice. Then He made school boards.

Following the Equator

To lead a life of undiscovered sin! That is true joy.

Society of American Authors

{REGARDING SATAN} We may not pay him reverence, for that would be indiscreet, but we can at least respect his talents.

Concerning the Jews

They was all Moslems, Tom said, and when I asked him what a Moslem was, he said it was a person that wasn't a Presbyterian. So there is plenty of them in Missouri, though I didn't know it before.

Tom Sawyer Abroad

{ON THE CONSCIENCE} It takes up more room than all the rest of a person's insides.

The Adventures of Huckleberry Finn

{ON MORALS} I'd rather teach them than practice them any day.

Morals and Memory

Profanity furnishes a relief denied even to prayer.

Attributed

There are two kinds of Christian morals, one private and the other public. These two are so distinct, so unrelated, that they are no more akin to each other than are archangels and politicians.

Taxes and Morals

French morality is not of that straight-laced description which is shocked at trifles.

Innocents Abroad

In statesmanship get the formalities right, never mind about the moralities.

Following the Equator

When angry, count four; when very angry, swear.

Pudd'nhead Wilson

He was a preacher . . . and never charged nothing for his preaching, and it was worth it, too.

The Adventures of Huckleberry Finn

Grown people everywhere are always likely to cling to the religion they were brought up in.

Following the Equator

{ASKED ABOUT HIS BELIEFS REGARDING HEAVEN AND HELL} You will excuse me if I remain silent on the matter. You see, I have friends in both places.

Attributed

I have no special regard for Satan; but I can at least claim that I have no prejudice against him. It may be that I lean a little his way, on account of his not having a fair show.

Concerning the Jews

There are those who scoff at the school-boy, calling him frivolous and shallow. Yet it was the school-boy who said, "Faith is believing what you know ain't so."

Following the Equator

Few sinners are saved after the first twenty minutes of a sermon.

Attributed

{ON HIS BOYHOOD DREAMS} Now and then we had a hope that if we lived and were good, God would permit us to be pirates.

Life on the Mississippi

Mark Twain

On Progress in Its
Many Splendid Forms

Soap and education are not as sudden as a massacre, but they are more deadly in the long run.

The Facts Concerning the Recent Resignation

Everybody talks about the weather, but nobody does anything about it.

Attributed

If I were to guess offhand, and without collusion with higher minds, what is the bottom cause of the amazing material and intellectual advancement of the last fifty years, I should guess that it was the modern-born and previously non-existent disposition on the part of men to believe that a new idea can have value.

A Majestic Literary Fossil

I see no great difference between a man and a watch, except that the man is conscious and the watch isn't, and the man tries to plan things and the watch doesn't.

The Turning-Point of My Life

I have entirely stopped using the typewriter, for the reason that I never could write a letter with it to anybody without receiving a request by return mail that I would not only describe the machine, but state what progress I had made in the use of it.

The First Writing-Machines

We are of one common superstition—the superstition that we realize the changes that are daily taking place in the world because we read about them and know what they are.

About All Kinds of Ships

I must have a prodigious quantity of mind; it takes me as much as a week sometimes to make it up.

Innocents Abroad

I lived in Hannibal fifteen and a half years, altogether, then ran away, according to the custom of persons who are intending to become celebrated.

Is Shakespeare Dead?

The radical invents the views. When he has worn them out, the conservative adopts them.

Notebook

Scientists have odious manners, except when you prop up their theory; then you can borrow money of them.

The Bee

{CONCERNING LEARNING TO RIDE THE BICYCLE} It is not like studying German, where you mull along, in a groping, uncertain way, for thirty years; and at last, just as you think you've got it, they spring the subjunctive on you, and there you are. No—and I see now, plainly enough, that the great pity about the German language is, that you can't fall off it and hurt yourself.

Taming the Bicycle

There are those who imagine that the unlucky accidents of life— life's "experiences"—are in some way useful to us. I wish I could find out how. I never knew one of them to happen twice.

Taming the Bicycle

Loyalty to petrified opinions never yet broke a chain or freed a human soul in this world—and never will.

Consistency

Between believing a thing and thinking you know is only a small step and quickly taken.

3,000 Years among the Microbes

Civilization: A limitless multiplication of unnecessary necessaries.

Attributed

Out of the public school grows the greatness of a nation.

Public Education

People always progress. You are better than your fathers and grandfathers were (this is the first time I have ever aimed a measureless slander at the departed . . .).

Plymouth Rock and the Pilgrims

I would rather have my ignorance than another man's knowledge, because I have got so much more of it.

Letter

≫≪

There should be a limit to public-school instruction; it cannot be wise or well to let the young find out everything.

English as She is Taught

≫≪

Habit is habit, and not to be flung out of the window by any man, but coaxed down-stairs a step at a time.

Pudd'nhead Wilson

≫≪

I have been in turn reporter, editor, publisher, author, lawyer, burglar. I have worked my way up, and wish to continue to do so.

Speech on Literature

≫≪

I have never let my schooling interfere with my education.

Attributed

Change is the handmaiden Nature requires to do her miracles with.

Roughing It

✕

It takes some little time to accept and realize the fact that while you have been growing old, your friends have not been standing still in the matter.

Life on the Mississippi

✕

A full belly is little worth where the mind is starved.

The Prince and the Pauper

✕

The man with a new idea is a Crank until the idea succeeds.

Following the Equator

✕

It always happens that when a man seizes upon a neglected and important idea, people inflamed with the same notion crop up all around.

Life on the Mississippi

That is just the way with some people. They get down on a thing when they don't know nothing about it.

The Adventures of Huckleberry Finn

My memory was never loaded with anything but blank cartridges.

Life on the Mississippi

Necessity is the mother of "taking chances."

Roughing It

There ain't no way to find out why a snorer can't hear himself snore.

Tom Sawyer Abroad

A scientist will never show any kindness for a theory which he did not start himself.

A Tramp Abroad

There's another trouble about theories: there's always a hole in them somewheres, sure, if you look close enough.

Tom Sawyer Abroad

It's noble to teach oneself. It is still nobler to teach others, and less trouble.

Doctor Van Dyke

On the Grim Reaper

I have achieved my seventy years in the usual way: by sticking strictly to a scheme of life which would kill anybody else.

Seventieth Birthday

I did not attend his funeral; but I wrote a nice letter saying I approved of it.

Attributed

{IN RESPONSE TO A NEWSPAPER ARTICLE CLAIMING HE WAS DYING}
I would not do such a thing at my time of life.

Death of Jean

Why is it that we rejoice at birth and grieve at a funeral? It is because we are not the person involved.

Pudd'nhead Wilson

Of necessity, an Obituary is a thing which cannot be so judiciously edited by any hand as by that of the subject of it.

Amended Obituaries

One million of us . . . die annually. Out of this million ten or twelve thousand are stabbed, shot, drowned, hanged, poisoned, or meet similarly violent death in some other way, such as perishing by kerosene-lamp and hoop-skirt conflagrations, getting buried in coal-mines, falling off house-tops, breaking through church or lecture-room floors, taking patent medicines, or committing suicide in other forms . . . And the rest of that million, amounting to the appalling figure of 987,631 corpses, die naturally in their beds! You will excuse me from taking any more chances on those beds.

The Danger of Lying in Bed

Whoever has lived long enough to find out what life is, knows how deep a debt of gratitude we owe to Adam, the first great benefactor of our race. He brought death into the world.

Pudd'nhead Wilson

{TWAIN ONCE TOLD AN INTERVIEWER THAT HIS FAMILY WASN'T SURE THAT HIS BROTHER BILL WAS DEAD, THOUGH HE HAD BEEN BURIED. TWAIN WENT ON TO EXPLAIN} You see, we were twins—defunct and I—and we got mixed in the bathtub when we were only two weeks old, and one of us was drowned. But we didn't know which. Some think it was Bill. Some think it was me.

An Encounter with an Interviewer

{TWAIN'S SUGGESTED EPITAPH FOR A LADY'S BELOVED MAID-SERVANT
WHO HAD FALLEN ASLEEP ON A STOVE AND BEEN ROASTED TO DEATH}
Well done, good and faithful servant.

Riley—Newspaper Correspondent

I have always felt that I should be hanged some day, and
somehow the thought has annoyed me considerably . . .

Lionizing Murderers

{TWAIN CLAIMED TO HAVE ACTED AS SECOND IN A DUEL, WHEN THE
OTHER SECOND SUGGESTED SMALL DUELING PISTOLS AT SIXTY-FIVE
YARDS, TWAIN REPLIED} Sixty-five yards, with these instruments?
Squirt-guns would be deadlier at fifty. Consider, my friend, you
and I are banded together to destroy life, not make it eternal.

A Tramp Abroad

I am hurt all over, but I cannot tell the full extent yet, because
the doctor is not done taking inventory. He will make out my
manifest this evening. However, thus far he thinks only sixteen
of my wounds are fatal. I don't mind the others.

Niagara

All say, "How hard it is that we have to die"—a strange complaint to come from the mouths of people who have had to live.

Pudd'nhead Wilson

I wish to urge upon you this—which I think is wisdom— that if you find you can't make seventy by any but an uncomfortable road, don't you go.

Seventieth Birthday

Let us endeavor so to live that when we come to die even the undertaker will be sorry.

Pudd'nhead Wilson

Much as the modern French duel is ridiculed by certain smart people, it is in reality one of the most dangerous institutions of our day. Since it is always fought in the open air the combatants are nearly sure to catch cold.

A Tramp Abroad

Pity is for the living, envy is for the dead.

Following the Equator

In order to know a community, one must observe the style of its funerals and know what manner of men they bury with most ceremony.

Roughing It

{ON THE RESULTS OF A GUNFIGHT} The next instant he was one of the deadest men that ever lived.

Roughing It

He has been a doctor a year now, and has had two patients—no, three, I think; yes, it was three. I attended their funerals.

The Gilded Age

Reports of my death are greatly exaggerated.

Attributed

Mark Twain

On Storytelling,
Writing, and Other Lies

I am not one of those who in expressing opinions confine themselves to facts.

Savage Club Dinner

How often we recall, with regret, that Napoleon once shot at a magazine editor and missed him and killed a publisher. But we remember with charity, that his intentions were good.

Letter

Broadly speaking, genius is not born with sight, but blind; and it is not itself that opens its eyes, but the subtle influences of a myriad of stimulating exterior circumstances.

Saint Joan of Arc

It is a curious thing, the currency that an idiotic saying can get. The man that first says it thinks he has made a discovery. The man he says it to, thinks the same. It departs on its travels, is received everywhere with admiring acceptance, and not only as a piece of rare and acute observation, but as being exhaustively true and profoundly wise; and so it presently takes its place in the world's list of recognized and established wisdoms.

Does the Race of Man Love a Lord?

Persons attempting to find a motive in this narrative will be prosecuted; persons attempting to find a moral in it will be banished; persons attempting to find a plot will be shot.

Preface to The Adventures of Huckleberry Finn

That is the way with art, when it is not acquired but born to you: you start in to make some simple little thing, not suspecting that your genius is beginning to work and swell and strain in secret, and all of a sudden there is a convulsion and you fetch out something astonishing.

How to Make History Dates Stick

The more you try to think of an unthinkable thing the more it eludes you.

How to Make History Dates Stick

There is only one expert who is qualified to examine the souls and the life of a people and make a valuable report—the native novelist. This expert is so rare that the most populous country can never have fifteen conspicuously and confessedly competent ones in stock at a time.

What Paul Bourget Thinks of Us

Use the right word, not its second cousin.

Fenimore Cooper's Literary Offenses

One of the most striking differences between a cat and a lie is that a cat has only nine lives.

Pudd'nhead Wilson

{ON A PARTICULARLY ARGUMENTATIVE RIVER BOAT PILOT TWAIN WORKED UNDER} He did his arguing with heat . . . and I did mine with the reserve and moderation of a subordinate who does not like to be flung out of a pilot-house that is perched forty feet above the water.

Is Shakespeare Dead?

{TWAIN'S DEFINITION OF A CLASSIC} Something everybody wants to have read and nobody wants to read.

Disappearance of Literature

Eloquence is the essential thing in a speech, not information.

3,000 Years among the Microbes

By some subtle law all tragic human experiences gain in pathos
by the perspective of time.

My Debut as a Literary Person

Experience is an author's most valuable asset; experience is the
thing that puts the muscle and the breath and the warm blood
into the book he writes.

Is Shakespeare Dead?

I always have the disposition to tell what is not so; I was born
with it; we all have it.

To My Missionary Critics

There are three infallible ways of pleasing an author . . . 1, to
tell him you have read one of his books; 2, to tell him you
have read all of his books; 3, to ask him to let you read the
manuscript of his forthcoming book. No. 1 admits you to his
respect; No. 2 admits you to his admiration; No. 3 carries you
clear into his heart.

Pudd'nhead Wilson

It is a good thing, perhaps, to write for the amusement of the public, but it is a far higher and nobler thing to write for their instruction, their profit, their actual and tangible benefit.

Curing a Cold

{TWAIN'S RESPONSE TO A LETTER ADDRESSED TO THE NEWSPAPER WHERE HE WORKED} Although we are now strangers, I feel we shall cease to be so if we ever become acquainted with each other.

Information for the Millions

{ON *WEBSTER'S DICTIONARY*) I have studied it often, but I never could discover the plot.

Attributed

I am not the editor of a newspaper, and shall always try to do right and be good, so that God will not make me one.

Letter

As to the Adjective: when in doubt, strike it out.

Pudd'nhead Wilson

I have been cautioned to talk but be careful not to say anything. I do not consider this a difficult task.

Nineteenth Century Progress

An injurious truth has no merit over an injurious lie. Neither should ever be uttered.

On the Decaying Art of Lying

She had exactly the German way; whatever was in her mind to be delivered, whether a mere remark, or a sermon, or a cyclopedia, or the history of a war, she would get it into a single sentence or die. Whenever the literary German dives into a sentence, that is the last you are going to see of him till he emerges on the other side of his Atlantic with his verb in his mouth.

A Connecticut Yankee in King Arthur's Court

With a hundred words to do it with, the literary artisan could catch that airy thought and tie it down and reduce it to a concrete condition, visible, substantial, understandable and all right, like a cabbage; but the artist does it with twenty, and the result is a flower.

William Dean Howells

{ACCORDING TO TWAIN THE INTRODUCTION HE RECEIVED FOR HIS FIRST SPEECH WAS MADE BY A MINER HE'D NEVER MET. THE MINER SAID} I don't know anything about this man. Anyhow, I only know two things about him. One is, he has never been to jail, and the other is, I don't know why.

Compliments and Degrees

I thoroughly believe that any man who's got anything worthwhile to say will be heard if he only says it often enough.

A Humorist's Confession

I have always had an idea that I was well equipped to write plays, but I have never encountered a manager who has agreed with me.

Speech made at the dramatization of *Pudd'nhead Wilson*

A man is always better than his printed opinions. A man always reserves to himself on the inside a purity and an honesty and a justice that are a credit to him, whereas the things that he prints are just the reverse.

Hamilton W. Mabie

{RESPONDING TO AN INTRODUCTION AS ONE OF THE WORLD'S GREATEST AUTHORS} I was sorry to have my name mentioned as one of the great authors, because they have a sad habit of dying off. Chaucer is dead, Spenser is dead, so is Milton, so is Shakespeare, and I am not feeling very well myself.

Statistics

There are only two forces that can carry light to all the corners of the globe—only two—the sun in the heavens and the Associated Press down here. I may seem to be flattering the sun, but I do not mean it so . . .

Spelling and Pictures

I don't know anything that mars good literature so completely as too much truth.

Savage Club Dinner

{TWAIN OFFERED THIS AS AN EXAMPLE OF FRANKLIN'S WIT AND WISDOM} Never put off till to-morrow what you can do day after to-morrow just as well.

The Late Benjamin Franklin

Get your facts first, and then you can distort 'em as much as you please.

Attributed

It usually takes me three weeks to prepare an impromptu speech.

Attributed

When it comes down to pure ornamental cursing, the native American is gifted above the sons of men.

Roughing It

War talk by men who have been in a war is always interesting; whereas moon talk by a poet who has not been in the moon is likely to be dull.

Life on the Mississippi

{ON GOSSIP} There is a lot to say in her favor, but the other is more interesting.

Attributed

Be careful about reading health books. You may die of a misprint.

Attributed

Against the assault of humor nothing can stand.

The Mysterious Stranger

"Let a sleeping dog lie." Right. Still when there is much at stake it is better to get a newspaper to do it.

Following the Equator

Why shouldn't truth be stranger than fiction? Fiction, after all, has to stick to possibilities.

Following the Equator

My own luck has been curious all my literary life; I never could tell a lie that anyone would doubt, nor a truth that anybody would believe.

Following the Equator

When in doubt, tell the truth.

Following the Equator

{IN RESPONSE TO A TOAST REFERRING TO ONE OF HIS MOST COMMONLY REPEATED AXIOMS "WHEN IN DOUBT, TELL THE TRUTH"} That maxim I did invent, but never expected it to be applied to me. I did say, "When you are in doubt," but when I am in doubt myself I use more sagacity.

When in Doubt, Tell the Truth

{TWAIN DISLIKED THE FREQUENT USE OF PARENTHETICAL STATEMENTS} It reminds a person of those dentists who secure your instant and breath less interest in a tooth by taking a grip on it with the forceps, and then stand there and drawl through a tedious anecdote before they give the dreaded jerk. Parentheses in literature and dentistry are in bad taste.

The Awful German Language

It is my conviction that one cannot get out of finely wrought literature all that is in it by reading it mutely.

William Dean Howells

I need not enlarge upon the influence the drama has exerted upon civilization. It has made good morals entertaining.

Henry Irving

[THE AUTHOR] has a fine gift in the matter of surprises; but as a rule they are not pleasant ones . . .

A Cure for the Blues

To believe that such talk ever came out of people's mouths would be to believe that there was a time when time was of no value to a person who thought he had something to say; when a man's mouth was a rolling-mill, and busied itself all day long in turning four-foot pigs of thought into thirty-foot bars of conversational railroad iron by attenuation.

Fenimore Cooper's Literary Offenses

I have a prejudice against people who print things in a foreign language and add no translation. When I am the reader, and the other considers me able to do the translating myself, he pays me quite a nice compliment—but if he would do the translating for me I would try to get along without the compliment.

A Tramp Abroad

The Critic

In the matter of intellect, the difference between a Cooper Indian and the Indian that stands in front of the cigar-shop is not spacious.

Fenimore Cooper's Literary Offenses

[THE AUTHOR] does not make the mistake of being relevant on one page and irrelevant on another; he is irrelevant on all of them.

A Cure for the Blues

{REGARDING WAGNER'S OPERA *PARSIFAL*} The first act of three occupied two hours, and I enjoyed that in spite of the singing. . . . Singing! It does seem the wrong name to apply to it. Strictly described, it is a practising of difficult and unpleasant intervals, mainly.

At the Shrine of Saint Wagner

Every time a Cooper [character] is in peril, and absolute silence is worth four dollars a minute, he is sure to step on a dry twig. There may be a hundred handier things to step on, but that wouldn't satisfy Cooper. Cooper requires him to turn out and find a dry twig; and if he can't do it, go and borrow one.

Fenimore Cooper's Literary Offenses

[THE RULES OF LITERATURE] require that the author shall make the reader feel a deep interest in the personages of his tale and in their fate; and that he shall make the reader love the good people in the tale and hate the bad ones. But the reader of the Deerslayer tale dislikes the good people in it, is indifferent to the others, and wishes they would all get drowned together.

Fenimore Cooper's Literary Offenses

The author . . . this good soul, whose intentions are always better than his English.

A Cure for the Blues

Jane Austen's books, too, are absent from this library. Just that one omission alone would make a fairly good library out of a library that hadn't a book in it.

Following the Equator

It is easy to find fault, if one has that disposition. There was once a man who, not being able to find any other fault with his coal, complained that there were too many prehistoric toads in it.

Pudd'nhead Wilson

It seems to me that just in the ratio that our newspapers increase, our morals decay. The more newspapers, the worse morals.

License of the Press

Uhlic says Wagner despised "Jene plapperude musik," and therefore "Runs, trills, and schnorkel are discarded by him." I don't know what a schnorkel is, but now that I know it has been left out of these operas I have never missed so much in my life.

At the Shrine of Saint Wagner

He would come in and say he had changed his mind—which was a gilded figure of speech, because he hadn't any . . .

The Old-fashioned Printer

One mustn't criticize people on grounds where he can't stand perpendicular himself.

A Connecticut Yankee in King Arthur's Court

Perdition is full of Hotels better than the Benton.

Innocents Abroad

{On the tradition of hurling flowers at female performers as ovation} A sincere compliment is always grateful to a lady, so long as you don't try to knock her down with it.

Letter

{Twain's pledge upon becoming editor of the *Buffalo Express*} I shall always confine myself strictly to the truth, except when it is attended with inconvenience; I shall witheringly rebuke all forms of crime and misconduct, except when committed by the party inhabiting my own vest . . .

Salutatory

It is easy to find fault, if one has that disposition. There was once a man who, not being able to find any other fault with his coal, complained that there were too many prehistoric toads in it.

Pudd'nhead Wilson

Few things are harder to put up with than the annoyance of a good example.

Pudd'nhead Wilson

Whenever I enjoy anything in art it means that it is mighty poor.

At the Shrine of Saint Wagner

{IN AN OPEN LETTER TO COMMODORE VANDERBILT) Go and surprise the whole country by doing something right.

Letter

Wagner's music is better than it sounds.

Attributed

Mark Twain

On Law and Politics

We have a criminal justice system which is superior to any in the world; and its efficiency is only marred by the difficulty of finding twelve men every day who don't know anything and can't read.

Americans and the English

Public servants: Persons chosen by the people to distribute the graft.

Attributed

A king is a king by accident; the reason the rest of us are not kings is merely due to another accident; we are all made of the same clay, and it is a sufficiently poor quality.

A Memorable Assassination

I've been a statesman without salary for many years, and I have accomplished great and widespread good. I don't know that it has benefited anybody very much, even if it was good; but I do know that it hasn't harmed me very much, and it hasn't made me any richer.

Municipal Corruption

{COMMENTING UPON AN ANCIENT LEGAL DECISION} The difference between a bench of judges and a basket of vegetables was as yet so slight that we may say with all confidence that it didn't really exist.

Switzerland, Cradle of Liberty

There are laws to protect the freedom of the press' speech, but none that are worth anything to protect the people from the press.

License of the Press

I suppose all Democrats are on sociable terms with the devil.

Among the Spirits

{IN RESPONSE TO THE QUESTION "WHAT ARE THE SWEETEST WORDS IN THE WORLD?"} Not Guilty.

Mental Photographs

There is no distinctly American criminal class except Congress.

Following the Equator

{ON A DISPUTE BETWEEN AN INVENTOR AND HIS GOVERNMENT}
I know the inventor very well, and he has my sympathy.
This is friendship. But I am throwing my influence with
the government. This is politics.

The Austrian Edison Keeping School Again

I don't mind what the opposition say of me so long as they don't
tell the truth about me. But when they descend to telling the
truth about me I consider that this is taking an unfair advantage.

Speech made at a Republican rally

Laws are sand, customs are rock. Laws can be evaded and
punishment escaped, but an openly transgressed custom
brings sure punishment.

The Gorky Incident

{REGARDING THE INSANITY PLEA} Formerly, if you killed a
man, it was possible that you were insane—but now, if
you, having friends and money, kill a man, it is evidence
that you are a lunatic.

A New Crime

Customs do not concern themselves with right or wrong
or reason.

The Gorky Incident

The less there is to justify a traditional custom the harder it is
to get rid of it.

The Adventures of Tom Sawyer

A crime preserved in a thousand centuries ceases to be a crime,
and becomes a virtue.

Following the Equator

Let us abolish policemen who carry clubs and revolvers, and
put in a squad of poets armed to the teeth with poems on
Spring and Love.

Poets as Policemen

Principles aren't of much account . . . except at election-time.
After that you hang them up to let them season.

Municipal Corruption

No public interest is anything other or nobler than a massed accumulation of private interests.

Spelling and Pictures

Honor is a harder master than the law.

Welcome Home

I used to rob orchards; a thing which I would not do today—if the orchards were watched.

Savage Club Dinner

We have an insanity plea that would have saved Cain.

Americans and the English

No people in the world ever did achieve their freedom by goody-goody talk and moral suasion: it being immutable law that all revolutions that will succeed, must begin in blood, whatever may answer afterward.

A Connecticut Yankee in King Arthur's Court

All kings is mostly rapscallions.

The Adventures of Huckleberry Finn

{ON THE CONGRESS} Whiskey is carried into committee rooms in demijohns and carried out in demagogues.

Notebook

Hain't we got all the fools in town on our side? And hain't that a big enough majority in any town?

The Adventures of Huckleberry Finn

{ON FRANCE} The law says, in effect, "It is the business of the weak to get out of the way of the strong." We fine a cabman if he runs over a citizen; Paris fines the citizen for being run over.

A Tramp Abroad

That's the difference between governments and individuals. Governments don't care, individuals do.

A Tramp Abroad

The master minds of all nations, in all ages, have sprung in affluent multitude from the mass of the nations, and from the mass of the nation only—not from its privileged classes.

A Connecticut Yankee in King Arthur's Court

Reader, suppose you were an idiot. And suppose you were a member of Congress. But I repeat myself.

Attributed

Custom supersedes all other forms of law.

Following the Equator

Speaking of burglars . . . I am disposed to allow them credit for whatever good qualities they possess. Chief among these . . . is their great care while doing business to avoid disturbing people's sleep.

Books and Burglars

Mark Twain

In America and Abroad!

I think there is but a single specialty with us, only one thing can be called by the wide name "American." That is the national devotion to ice-water.

What Paul Bourget Thinks of Us

{ON THE EMPRESS OF AUSTRO-HUNGARY AFTER HER ASSASSINATION} Crowns have adorned others, but she adorned her crowns.

A Memorable Assassination

If there were an earthquake in Berlin the police would take charge of it and conduct it in that sort of orderly way that would make you think it was a prayer-meeting.

The German Chicago

{ON THE ITALIANS} They spell it Vinci, but pronounce it Vinchy. Foreigners always spell better than they pronounce.

Innocents Abroad

Guides cannot master the subtleties of the American joke.

Innocents Abroad

The cross of the Legion of Honour has been conferred upon me. However, few escape that distinction.

A Tramp Abroad

It is by the goodness of God that in our country we have those three unspeakably precious things: freedom of speech, freedom of conscience, and the prudence never to practice either of them.

Following the Equator

The awful power, the public opinion of a nation, is created in America by a hoard of ignorant, self-complacent simpletons who railed at ditching and shoemaking and fetched up journalism on their way to the poorhouse.

License of the Press

{TWAIN'S ADVICE TO SOLDIERS} When you leave a battlefield, always leave it in good order. Remove the wreck and rubbish and tidy up the place. However, in the case of a drawn battle it is neither party's business to tidy up anything—you can leave it looking as if the city government of New York had bossed the fight.

Instructing the Soldier

The Englishman requires that everything about him shall be stable, strong, and permanent, except the house which he builds to rent.

Letters to Satan

The crusty, ill-mannered and in every way detestable Parisian cabman ought to imitate our courteous and friendly Boston cabman—and stop there. He can't learn anything from the guild in New York.

Some National Stupidities

{TWAIN ON THE STATE OF NEVADA} There is a popular tradition that the Almighty created it; but when you come to see it . . . you will think differently.

Information for the Millions

[BENJAMIN FRANKLIN] was always proud of telling how he entered Philadelphia for the first time, with nothing in the world but two shillings in his pocket and four rolls of bread under his arm. But really, when you come to examine it critically, it was nothing. Anybody could have done it.

The Late Benjamin Franklin

Look out for rain. It would be absurd to look in for it.

A Page from a California Almanac

{REGARDING GEORGE WASHINGTON} As a boy, he gave no promise
of the greatness he was one day to achieve. He was ignorant
of the commonest accomplishments of youth. He could not
even lie.

A Brief Biographical Sketch of George Washington

{TWAIN ONCE TRIED TO SELL A BUCKING BRONCO, TO NO AVAIL}
Parties said earthquakes were handy enough on the Pacific
coast—they did not wish to own one.

Roughing It

{REGARDING NEW YORK CITY COMMUTERS} I reckon they'd tackle
a hearse, if it was going their way.

Roughing It

I have noticed that even the angels speak English with an accent.

Following the Equator

They keep always trying to make your bed before you get up, thus destroying your rest and inflicting agony upon you; but after you get up, they don't come any more till next day.

Concerning Chambermaids

It used to be a good hotel, but that proves nothing—I used to be a good boy, for that matter. Both of us have lost character of late years.

Innocents Abroad

{TWAIN ONCE ASKED FOR A LAMP TO READ BY AT A MEAGER HOTEL, THE PORTER BROUGHT HIM TWO SHORT, TALLOW CANDLES. TWAIN RESPONDED} Light them both—I'll have to have one to see the other by.

Innocents Abroad

The early twilight of a Sunday evening in Hamilton, Bermuda, is an alluring time. There is just enough of whispering breeze, fragrance of flowers, and sense of repose to raise one's thoughts heavenward; and just enough amateur piano music to keep him reminded of the other place.

Some Rambling Notes of an Idle Excursion

There are several "sights" in the Bermudas, of course, but they are easily avoided. This is a great advantage—one cannot have it in Europe.

Some Rambling Notes of an Idle Excursion

{Regarding the city of Belfast, Ireland} Every man in the community is a missionary and carries a brick to admonish the erring with.

"Party Cries" in Ireland

{Regarding the weather in New England} There is only one thing certain about it: you are certain there is going to be plenty of it . . .

Speech on the Weather

{Regarding an alleged ancestor of Twain's who was banished to Rhode Island} Recognizing that this was really carrying harshness to an unjustifiable extreme, they took pity on him and burned him.

Plymouth Rock and the Pilgrims

German books are easy enough to read when you hold them before the looking-glass or stand on your head . . .

The Awful German Language

I heard a Californian student in Heidelberg say, in one of his calmest moods, that he would rather decline two drinks than one German adjective.

The Awful German Language

{ON FRENCH WAITERS} They know English; that is, they know it on the European plan—which is to say, they can speak it, but can't understand it.

Paris Notes

{ON THE VIRTUE OF CONSIDERATION} Is it an American characteristic? So far as I have observed, the most prominent, the most American of all American characteristics, is the poverty of it in the American character.

Doctor Van Dyke

The coldest winter I ever spent was a summer in San Francisco.

Attributed to Twain by the Mark Twain Hotel, San Francisco

The objects of which Paris folks are fond—literature, art, medicine, and adultery.

The Corpse

There are many humorous things in the world; among them, the white man's notion that he is less savage than the other savages.

Following the Equator

Even popularity can be overdone. In Rome, along at first, you are full of regrets that Michelangelo died; but by and by you only regret that you didn't see him do it.

Pudd'nhead Wilson

Behold America, the refuge of the oppressed from everywhere (who can pay fifty dollars' admission) . . .

China and the Philippines

Patriotism is usually the refuge of the scoundrel. He is the man who talks the loudest.

Education and Citizenship

{ON THE SEA PASSAGE FROM NEW YORK TO ENGLAND} I have gone over that same route so often that I know my way without a compass, just by the waves. I know all the large waves and a good many of the small ones. Also the sunsets. I know every sunset and where it belongs just by its color.

An Undelivered Speech

{REGARDING LONDON} I stop a citizen and say: "How far is it to Charing Cross?" "Shilling fare in a cab," and off he goes. I suppose if I were to ask a Londoner how far it is from the sublime to the ridiculous, he would try to express it in coin.

About London

In Boston they ask, "How much does he know?" In New York, "How much is he worth?" In Philadelphia, "Who were his parents?"

What Paul Bourget Thinks of Us

Ours is the "land of the free"—nobody denies that—nobody challenges it. (Maybe it is because we won't let other people testify.)

Roughing It

Twenty-four years ago I was strangely handsome; in San Francisco in the rainy season I was often mistaken for fair weather.

Attributed

Travel is fatal to prejudice, bigotry, and narrow-mindedness, and many of our people need it sorely on these accounts. Broad, wholesome, charitable views of men and things cannot be acquired by vegetating in one little corner of the earth all one's lifetime.

Innocents Abroad

I believe that in India "cold weather" is merely a conventional phrase . . . to distinguish between weather which will melt a brass door-knob and weather which will only make it mushy.

Following the Equator

Names are not always what they seem. The common Welsh name Bzjxxlwcp is pronounced Jackson.

Following the Equator

A street in Constantinople is a picture which one ought to see once—not oftener.

Innocents Abroad

{REGARDING BENJAMIN FRANKLIN} He was twins, being born simultaneously in two different houses in the city of Boston. These houses remain unto this day, and have signs upon them worded in accordance with the fact.

The Late Benjamin Franklin

{RESPONDING TO FRENCH AUTHOR PAUL BOURGET'S CLAIM THAT HE HAS CHRONICLED "THE NATURE OF THE PEOPLE" OF THE UNITED STATES} We have been accused of being a nation addicted to inventing wild schemes. I trust we shall be allowed to retire to second place now.

What Paul Bourget Thinks of Us

{REGARDING BERMUDA} We never met a man, or woman, or child anywhere in this sunny island who seemed to be unprosperous, or discontented, or sorry about anything . . . The spectacle of an entire nation groveling in contentment is an infuriating thing.

Some Rambling Notes of an Idle Excursion

The building commissioners {in Berlin} inspect while the building is going up. It has been found that this is better than to wait till it falls down.

The German Chicago

At bottom he was probably fond of them [the Americans], but he was always able to conceal it.

My First Lie, And How I Got Out of It

Mark Twain

On Food, Smoking, and
Life's Little Pleasures

I smoke a good deal—that is to say, all the time.

Mental Telegraphy

In the presence of bilge-water, Limburger cheese becomes odorless and ashamed.

About All Kinds of Ships

{REGARDING A PARTICULARLY DISGUSTING MENU} The wide intervals of the bill {of fare} were packed with dishes calculated to insult a cannibal.

At the Appetite Cure

Vienna Coffee! . . . That sumptuous coffee-house coffee, compared with which all other European and all American hotel coffee is mere fluid poverty.

At the Appetite Cure

Training is everything. . . . Cauliflower is nothing but cabbage with a college education.

Pudd'nhead Wilson

{Referring to quitting smoking} I've done it a hundred times!

Attributed

As an example to others, and not that I care for moderation myself, it has always been my rule never to smoke when asleep, and never to refrain when awake.

Seventieth Birthday

[I] came into the world asking for a light.

Concerning Tobacco

Of all the unchristian beverages that ever passed my lips, Turkish coffee is the worst.

Innocents Abroad

They ran up the Cannibal flag and had a grand human barbecue in honor of it, in which it was noticed that the better a man liked a friend the better he enjoyed him.

Riley—Newspaper Correspondent

{ACTING AS FASHION CORRESPONDENT FOR HIS NEWSPAPER} She had a beautiful complexion when she first came, but it faded out by degrees in an unaccountable way. However, it is not lost for good. I found the most of it on my shoulder afterward.

A Fashion Item

{REGARDING "SELF-PLEASURE"} Of all the various kinds of sexual intercourse this has least to recommend it. As an amusement it is too fleeting. As an occupation it is too wearing. As a public exhibition, there is no money in it.

The Science of Onanism

What work I have done I have done because it has been play. If it had been work I shouldn't have done it.

A Humorist's Confession

The true Southern watermelon is a boon apart, and not to be mentioned with commoner things. . . . When one has tasted it, he knows what the angels eat. It was not a Southern watermelon that Eve took; we know it because she repented.

Pudd'nhead Wilson

{ON CLOTHING} They are on us to expose us—to advertise what we wear them to conceal.

Following the Equator

Some civilized women would lose half their charm without dress, and some would lose all of it.

The Dress of Civilized Women

What, sir, would the people of the earth be without woman? They would be scarce, sir, almighty scarce.

Woman—An Opinion

Part of the secret of success in life is to eat what you like and let the food fight it out inside.

Attributed

A man accustomed to American food and American cookery would not starve to death suddenly in Europe; but I think he would gradually waste away, and eventually die.

A Tramp Abroad

{TWAIN'S ADVICE TO THE GRADUATING CLASS OF ST. TIMOTHY'S SCHOOL FOR GIRLS} First, girls, don't smoke—that is, don't smoke to excess . . . Second, don't drink—that is, don't drink to excess . . . Third, don't marry—I mean, to excess.

Advice to Girls

I have known the horse in war and peace, and there is no place where a horse is comfortable. The horse has too many caprices, and he is too much given to initiative. He invents too many new ideas.

Welcome Home

{REGARDING HAWAII} At noon I observed a bevy of nude native young ladies bathing in the sea, and went and sat down on their clothes to keep them from being stolen.

Roughing It

{A DESCRIPTION OF TWAIN'S PECULIAR DANCING} I . . . polkaed and scotisched with a step peculiar to myself—and the kangaroo.

Roughing It

I smoke in moderation, only one cigar at a time.

Advice to Girls

Golf is a good walk spoiled.

Attributed

I would rather go to bed with Lillian Russell stark naked than Ulysses S. Grant in full military regalia.

Attributed

The Germans are exceedingly fond of Rhine wines. . . . One tells them from vinegar by the label.

A Tramp Abroad

The only way to keep your health is to eat what you don't want, drink what you don't like, and do what you'd druther not.

Following the Equator

On the Continent, you can't get a rare beefsteak—everything is as overdone as a martyr.

Notebook

Ours was a reasonably comfortable ship, with the customary seagoing fare—plenty of good food furnished by the Deity and cooked by the Devil.

Following the Equator

Don't part with your illusions. When they are gone, you may still exist, but you have ceased to live.

Following the Equator

Seventieth Birthday
(excerpt)

Excerpt from an Address at a Dinner Given by Colonel George Harvey at Delmonico's, December 5, 1905, to Celebrate the Seventieth Anniversary of Mr. Clemens' Birth:

This is my seventieth birthday, and I wonder if you all rise to the size of that proposition, realizing all the significance of that phrase, seventieth birthday.

The seventieth birthday! It is the time of life when you arrive at a new and awful dignity; when you may throw aside the decent reserves which have oppressed you for a generation and stand unafraid and unabashed upon your seven-terraced summit and look down and teach—unrebuked: You can tell the world how you got there. It is what they all do. You shall never get tired of telling by what delicate arts and deep moralities you climbed up to that great place. You will explain the process and dwell on the particulars with senile rapture. I have been anxious to explain my own system this long time, and now at last I have the right.

I have achieved my seventy years in the usual way: by sticking strictly to a scheme of life which would kill anybody else. It sounds like an exaggeration, but that is really the common rule for attaining to old age. When we examine the programme of any of these garrulous old people we always find that the habits which have preserved them would have decayed us; that the way of life which enabled them to live upon the property of their heirs so long, as Mr. Choate says, would have put us out of commission ahead of time. I will offer here, as a sound maxim, this: That we can't reach old age by another man's road.

I will now teach, offering my way of life to whomsoever desires to commit suicide by the scheme which has enabled me to beat the doctor and the hangman for seventy years. Some of the details may sound untrue, but they are not. I am not here to deceive; I am here to teach.

We have no permanent habits until we are forty. Then they begin to harden, presently they petrify, then business begins. Since forty I have been regular about going to bed and getting up—and that is one of the main things. I have made it a rule to go to bed when there wasn't anybody left to sit up with; and I have made it a rule to get up when I had to. This has resulted in an unswerving regularity of irregularity. It has saved me sound, but it would injure another person.

In the matter of diet—which is another main thing—I have been persistently strict in sticking to the things which didn't agree with me until one or the other of us got the best of it. Until lately I got the best of it myself. But last spring I stopped frolicking with mince-pie after midnight; up to then I had always believed it wasn't loaded. For thirty years I have taken coffee and bread at eight in the morning, and no bite nor sup until seven-thirty in the evening. Eleven hours. That is all right for me, and is wholesome, because I have never had a headache in my life, but headachy people would not reach seventy comfortably by that road, and they would be foolish to try it. And I urge upon you this—which I think is wisdom—that if you find you can't make seventy by any but an uncomfortable road, don't you go. When they take off the Pullman and retire you to the rancid smoker, put on your things, count your checks, and get out at the first way station where there's a cemetery.

I have made it a rule never to smoke more than one cigar at a time. I have no other restriction as regards smoking. I do not know just when I began to smoke, I only know that it was in my father's lifetime, and that I was discreet. He passed from this life early in 1847, when I was a shade past eleven; ever since then I have smoked publicly. As an example to others, and not that I care for moderation myself, it has always been my rule never to smoke when asleep, and never to refrain when awake. It is a good rule. I mean, for me; but some of you know quite well that it wouldn't answer for everybody that's trying to get to be seventy.

I smoke in bed until I have to go to sleep; I wake up in the night, sometimes once, sometimes twice, sometimes three times, and I never waste any of these opportunities to smoke. This habit is so old and dear and precious to me that I would feel as you, sir, would feel if you should lose the only moral you've got—meaning the chairman—if you've got one: I am making no charges. I will grant, here, that I have stopped smoking now and then, for a few months at a time, but it was not on principle, it was only to show off, it was to pulverize those critics who said I was a slave to my habits and couldn't break my bonds.

To-day it is all of sixty years since I began to smoke the limit. I have never bought cigars with life-belts around them. I early found that those were too expensive for me. I have always bought cheap cigars—reasonably cheap, at any rate. Sixty years ago they cost me four dollars a barrel, but my taste has improved; latterly, and I pay seven now. Six or seven. Seven, I think, Yes; it's seven. But that includes the barrel. I often have smoking parties at my house; but the people that come have always just taken the pledge. I wonder why that is?

As for drinking, I have no rule about that. When the others drink I like to help; otherwise I remain dry, by habit and preference. This dryness does not hurt me, but it could easily hurt you, because you are different. You let it alone.

Since I was seven years old I have seldom taken a dose of medicine, and have still seldomer needed one. But up to seven

I lived exclusively on allopathic medicines. Not that I needed them, for I don't think I did; it was for economy; my father took a drug-store for a debt, and it made cod-liver oil cheaper than the other breakfast foods. We had nine barrels of it, and it lasted me seven years. Then I was weaned. The rest of the family had to get along with rhubarb and ipecac and such things, because I was the pet. I was the first Standard Oil Trust. I had it all. By the time the drug-store was exhausted my health was established, and there has never been much the matter with me since. But you know very well it would be foolish for the average child to start for seventy on that basis. It happened to be just the thing for me, but that was merely an accident; it couldn't happen again in a century.

I have never taken any exercise, except sleeping and resting, and I never intend to take any. Exercise is loathsome. And it cannot be any benefit when you are tired; and I was always tired. But let another person try my way, and see where he will come out.

I desire now to repeat and emphasize that maxim: We can't reach old age by another man's road. My habits protect my life, but they would assassinate you.

I have lived a severely moral life. But it would be a mistake for other people to try that, or for me to recommend it. Very few would succeed: you have to have a perfectly colossal stock of morals; and you can't get them on a margin; you have to have the whole thing, and put them in your box. Morals are an acquirement—like music, like a foreign language, like piety, poker, paralysis—no man is born with them. I wasn't myself, I started poor. I hadn't a single moral. There is hardly a man in this house that is poorer than I was then. Yes, I started like that—the world before me, not a moral in the slot. Not even an insurance moral. I can remember the first one I ever got. I can remember the landscape, the weather, the—I can remember how everything looked. It was an old moral, an old second-hand moral, all out of repair, and didn't fit, anyway. But if you are careful with a thing like that, and keep it in a dry place, and save it for processions, and Chautauquas, and World's Fairs, and so on, and disinfect it now and then, and give it a fresh coat of whitewash once in a while, you will be surprised to see how well she will last and how long she will keep sweet, or at least inoffensive. When I got that mouldy old moral, she had stopped growing, because she hadn't any exercise; but I worked her hard, I worked her Sundays and all. Under this cultivation she waxed in might and stature beyond belief, and served me well and was my pride and joy for sixty-three years; then she got to associating with insurance presidents, and lost flesh and character, and was a sorrow to look at and no longer competent for business. She was a great loss to me. Yet not all loss. I sold her—ah, pathetic skeleton, as she was—I sold her to Leopold, the pirate King of Belgium; he sold her to our Metropolitan Museum, and it was very glad to get her, for with out a rag on, she stands 57 feet long and 16 feet high, and they think she's a brontosaur. Well, she looks it. They believe it will take nineteen geological periods to breed her match. . . .

Threescore years and ten!

It is the Scriptural statute of limitations. After that, you owe no active duties; for you the strenuous life is over. You are a time-expired man, to use Kipling's military phrase: You have served your term, well or less well, and you are mustered out. You are become an honorary member of the republic, you are emancipated, compulsions are not for you, nor any bugle-call but "lights out." You pay the time-worn duty bills if you choose, or decline if you prefer—and without prejudice—for they are not legally collectable.

The previous-engagement plea, which in forty years has cost you so many twinges, you can lay aside forever; on this side of the grave you will never need it again. If you shrink at thought of night, and winter, and the late home-coming from the banquet and the lights and the laughter through the deserted streets—a desolation which would not remind you now, as for a generation it did, that your friends are sleeping, and you must creep in a-tiptoe and not disturb them, but would only remind you that you need not tiptoe, you can never disturb them more—if you shrink at thought of these things, you need only reply, "Your invitation honors me, and pleases me because you still keep me in your remembrance, but I am seventy; seventy, and would nestle in the chimney-corner, and smoke my pipe, and read my book, and take my rest, wishing you well in affection, and that when you in your return shall arrive at pier No. 70 you may step aboard your waiting ship with a reconciled spirit, and lay your course toward the sinking sun with a contented heart."

There is nothing much left of me but my age and my righteousness, but I leave with you my love and my blessing, and may you always keep your youth.